Woman's Aesthetic Mission

Jacob Von Falke and Helen Gorrill

Boom Academic Press
An imprint of Boom Publications Ltd
272 Bath Street
Glasgow SCOTLAND
G2 4JR

Boom Academic Press and the logo are trademarks of Boom Publications Ltd.

Boom Publications Ltd is a more-than-profit company, dedicating over half our profits to university scholarships for underprivileged students worldwide. In order to offset our carbon footprint, we also pledge to plant a tree for each graduation book commissioned.

Woman's Aesthetic Place
was first published in Great Britain in 1879, and subsequently reprinted as a Boom Publication in 2022.

Copyright of foreword © Helen Gorrill. Helen Gorrill has asserted her right under the Copyright, Designs and Patents Act, 1988,
to be identified as Author of this work.
For legal purposes any Acknowledgements constitute
an extension of this copyright page.
Cover design by Boom Academic Press and the Book Cover Zone USA.

All rights are reserved. No part of this publication may be reproduced or transmitted in any form or by any means, electronic or mechanical, including photocopying, recording, or any information storage or retrieval system, without prior permission in writing from the publishers.
Boom Publications Ltd do not have any control over, or responsibility for any third-party websites referred to or in this book. All internet addresses given in this book were correct at the time of going to press. The author and publisher regret any inconvenience if addresses have changed or sites have ceased to exist, but can accept no responsibility for any such changes.

Typeset by Helen at Boom Graduates.
Printed and bound in the UK.
To find out more about our authors and books visit www.boomgraduates.com
and sign up for our newsletters.

Woman's Aesthetic Mission

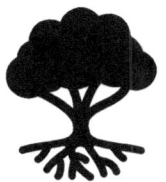

We plant a tree for every
Boom Academic Press book commissioned, and
thereafter plant a tree for every 10 books sold!

Watch our forest grow at
https://moretrees.eco/forest/BoomPublicationsLtd/

Jacob Von Falke and Helen Gorrill

Woman's Aesthetic Mission

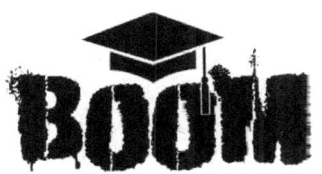

Jacob Von Falke and Helen Gorrill

Acknowledgements

With grateful thanks to DJCAD graduate of 2022, Maella Wallace. I was first introduced to Jacob Von Falke's 19th Century text by Maella in her brilliant dissertation 'A Critical Analysis of Gender and Identity through Contemporary Rug Making'. This illustrates the two-way learning process between dissertation supervisors and their students, and I shall be eternally grateful to Maella for educating me!

Jacob Von Falke and Helen Gorrill

FOREWORD

Helen Gorrill

2022

The text which follows – 'Women's Aesthetic Mission' - was originally published in 1879, the final chapter of a book named *Art in the House: Historical, Critical, and Aesthetical Studies on the Decoration and Furnishing of the Dwelling*. Written by Jacob Von Falke – a 19th Century 'tastemaker', curator and cultural commentator, the mission of the book was to educate men in how to best display – or monitor their wives in displaying – art collections, everyday objects and furniture in a pleasing fashion within the home. The book might therefore be considered an original tome of interior design, persuading homeowners to enhance, decorate, arrange and furnish their homes to achieve a more aesthetically pleasing environment for the people using the space. Moreover, almost 150 years old, the text offers a glimpse into the expected codes of conduct for gendered roles ascribed to men and women in the 19th Century.

It is the first clear text I have come across that succinctly states why women are incapable of many things, but in particular Von Falke addresses in this text why women should not be artists. However, we must ask ourselves, to what extent have things changed? There are surprising (and alarming) similarities between this 19th Century text and today's society, with the denigration of women's capabilities in both their creation of artworks, and the perceived limitations of their creative outputs.

It is poignant that Von Falke chooses to insert this final chapter directed at women – as an afterthought or a postscript. He states clearly that he aims to uncover the 'limits' of women's aesthetic mission. This aligns with work carried out by 19th Century Anthropologist and Psychologist Gustave Le Bon, whose main focus was to provide evidence that both women and non-European races were inferior to the white European male.

At the time of writing his book, Von Falke's 19th Century Western society focused on determining that women's allegedly smaller brains were proof of women's lesser mental capabilities. Flawed evidence was produced to show that women's brains were five ounces lighter than men's, and used to sustain men's rights to positions of power and influence. In *The Gendered Brain* (2019) Gina Rippon writes:

> There was to be no stone unturned (or skull unexamined) in the hunt for the proof of women's inferiority. One paper used over 5,000 measurements on a single skull. There were seemingly infinite ways of measuring the skull, with the focus on those that not only best differentiated men from women, but also ensured that women were reliably characterised as inferior, either childlike or similar to reviled 'lower' races.

In reading this historic text, we can see Von Falke perceived his role was to advise, but notably, to keep women in their place, due to their apparent biological inferiority. Perhaps we can understand although not excuse such a historic viewpoint in light of the contemporaneous political and social circumstances. However, we cannot excuse nor understand such attitudes towards women that prevail in the 21ˢᵗ Century – particularly within the artworld.

On reading this text for the first time, I recognised many parallels with what is happening in the artworld today – stemming from Linda Nochlin's 1971 paper 'Why have there been no great women artists?', and swathes of texts that followed through the 1980s and 1990s in the aftermath of the backlash that followed the struggles of the feminist art movement of the previous decade(s). In 2022, the world's bestselling art book – Ernst Gombrich's *Story of Art* – still contains only one woman artist out of hundreds of pages of men - and women are still annexed away or ghettoised in museums (for example, as we see at the Brooklyn Museum's Elizabeth Sackler Center for Feminist Art in New York).

Notably, in 2013 and 2015, the prominent German artist Georg Baselitz infamously stated 'Women simply cannot paint' (the statement which instigated my PhD and subsequent book *Women Can't paint: Gender, the Glass Ceiling and Values in Contemporary Art*, 2020). Prior to this *The Independent*'s art critic Brian Sewell declared that there is no such thing as a great woman artist. Copycat fledgling critics such as the contemporary British author Alexander Adams appear to align their views with those of white, male supremacy extremists. Therefore, as unbelievable as the following 19th Century text may read, it is poignant and crucial for students of today to understand it within the wider context of the artworld we have inherited, and one whose Victorian values prevail. In reading this text – 'Women's Aesthetic Mission' – it is important to consider the legacy of our

Victorian forefathers. Currently, in 2022 as I write this foreword, we have a 90 per cent gender pay (value) gap in the artworld – which means that for every £1 a man earns, women earn just 10p (Sieghart 2022). When men sign their artwork it goes up in value, yet when women sign art it goes down in value (Gørrill 2020). The vast majority of artwork collected by our great museums in their selection of work that will constitute the art history of the future - is made by men. Therefore we must ask ourselves, just how much of Von Falke's 1879 legacy still lingers today?

References

Gombrich, Ernst. 2007. *The Story of Art*. New York: Phaidon Press.

Gørrill, Helen. 2020. *Women Can't Paint: Gender, the Glass Ceiling and Values in Contemporary Art*. London & New York: Bloomsbury.

Nochlin, Linda. 1971. 'Why have there been no great women artists?'

Rippon, Gina. 2019. *The Gendered Brain*. London: Penguin.

Sieghart, Mary-Ann. 2022. 'Mind-blowing: Why do men's paintings cost ten times those of women?'. *The Guardian*. 2 August.

WOMAN'S AESTHETIC MISSION

Jacob Von Falke
1879

The Subject of Household Art cannot be said to have been adequately treated, even after the most exhaustive discussion of every decorative and useful object in the house, so long as we have not considered woman, its mistress, in her relation to it, and her artistic work. We must therefore endeavour to discover the aims as well as the limits, of her aesthetic mission.

Here some student of history may perhaps doubtingly ask, How can woman's aesthetic mission be discussed? The whole history of art clearly disproves it, since everything really great and beautiful which we know about, and everything which exists to charm our astonished gaze, is the creation of the stronger and not of the fairer portions of mankind. The temples of the Egyptians and Greeks, the gigantic domes of the Middle Ages, the sculptures of the Parthenon, the frescoes of the Vatican, and all the other monuments which, century after century, have been objects of pilgrimage to men of culture whose souls are ever searching for the land of beauty, sprang from the masculine brain, and were executed by man's hard hand.

It is true that history also records the names of women who have actively laboured in the wide domain of the arts of design, such as Sabina von Steinbach, Margaret van Eyck, Elizabetta Sirani,

Angelica Kaufmann, Rachel Ruysch, and many women of our own time whose names might be deservedly added to the list. But how small and limited is the field which they cultivated, how insignificant is their number as compared to that of the men who have worked in the same sphere of human activity, and how far in the background must we place their achievements, if we take into consideration grandeur of style, depth and breadth of conception, elevation and boldness of idea, exuberance of life, energy and vehemence of passion!

If we look over the whole broad field of art, we shall find that the hand of woman has laboured with success in but a very narrow portion of it. Instinctively true to her nature, she has preferred the minute and charming, the delicate and amiable, the tender and graceful, and has cultivated it diligently, lovingly, patiently, with talent and skill even, but yet in a humble style. On her own ground woman may compete for the prize with the hope of winning it, though, when we acknowledge that she is great in her speciality, we must perforce add, but her speciality is small.

As a matter of course, there are apparent as well as actual exceptions to this rule, although they are few in number. There are female sculptors, for instance, such as the Duchess Mary of Wurtemberg, the daughter of Louis Philippe, who did not shrink from handling the hammer and the chisel with her delicate hands, or from rough work in clay and stone. Nevertheless, when we look at her statue of the heroic Maid of Orleans, whom she represented as a pious visionary resigned to the will of God, though hardly heroic, we must own that after all the exception only proves the rule. While in this case the conception of the figure is superior to the execution, there are female painters, on the other hand, who work out their conceptions boldly and powerfully, with a broad touch, and, to use artistic language, with the hand of a virtuoso. While this expression, which is applicable only to man's work, implies (in woman) an overstepping of the bounds of nature, experience has also taught us that such female artists have very generally won their right to this title at the expense of especially feminine qualities in their domestic and social relations.

These remarks, however, are not at all intended to convey the idea that nature has forever shut out the intellect and the hand of woman from the field of high art; though, if we rely upon historical grounds, or look around us, we cannot avoid this conclusion. We must accept the fact that hitherto woman has been obliged to yield the laurels of high art to the hand of a competitor stronger than herself, and has as yet given no evidence of her capability of winning them. Let her not, however, despair of success in the future, and meanwhile let her look elsewhere for consolation.

In those branches of art, namely, which we generally call high art, although art is in reality one and indivisible, the whole realm of art or of beauty is not comprised. It is undoubtedly in them that the finest flower of culture and of all intellectual effort is to be found, and it is for this reason that we include them under the head of high art. Highly, however, as we may value the forms of art here referred to, their fruit is within the reach of a comparatively small number, for few are the fortunate mortals upon whom the joys which they bestow are abundantly showered. Shall the gates of the kingdom of beauty be therefore closed to the countless and to whom all possibility of coming under the influences of art is denied? Shall the mass of mankind have no part whatever in the blessings which are derived from the contemplation of works of art, and from commerce with the beautiful? By no means! The kingdom of beauty, if we admit that it is to be attained step by step, may perhaps be said to culminate in high art, but it certainly is not entered through it.

Below high art, if we must so call it, or, more correctly speaking, side by side with it, there is still a widespread domain which is governed by beauty, and in which the beautiful and the useful are united. It is sometimes called the realm of taste, although, in the present unfortunate condition of things for women, it would be more appropriate to call it the realm of man.

Why indeed should woman's occupation of adding beauty to the home appear trivial and unimportant because it is merely concerned with small things? Think for a moment how important the development of a love of beauty in the human mind has been considered to be throughout the whole course of history, and how important it is thought to be as a part of modern culture! Art, it is said, refines the manners, diverts our thoughts from low and vulgar things, consoles us for the many troubles and discomforts of material existence, and raises us above them into a higher spiritual sphere: it humanises us, and idealises our life. All this it does by awakening the aesthetic sense in us by increasing our pleasure in beauty and our capacity for its enjoyment, and by continually providing new food and new objects of delight to satisfy the longings which it has awakened. It would be a mistaken, however, to suppose that we can only be educated by works of high art. They do indeed specially promote the appreciation of beauty, but this can also be developed by small and comparatively unimportant objects, which are, after all, the only ones accessible to the vast majority of mankind, no less than by works of art of a monumental character.

We should therefore do wrong to despise that phase of beauty which they represent, or to undervalue and neglect its importance, and all the more because the objects alluded to are precisely those among which we grow up, from which, in early childhood, we receive our first impressions, and by which we are first impelled to cultivate the aesthetic sense. The child's first glance rests upon them, and his eyes become accustomed to them; he uses those objects which surround him; and which form part of his experiences. It lies, however, in their very nature, that being principally intended to please and attract by their outward beauty, these objects appeal much more readily to the growing mind of the child, and therefore aid him much more in his first steps toward aesthetic culture, than the great works of high art, for whose full enjoyment and comprehension a ripe understanding is above all things necessary. The importance of these objects of beauty is, however, not limited to childhood. For many years they are often the only ones which excite the aesthetic faculty in us and as they are the sole representatives of art in the house, their influence is perpetual. They do with us through life, and we are often obliged to rest content with them as our only source of aesthetic nourishment.

It has been said with trust that taste, or in other words, the sense of beauty, that is, the faculty of distinguishing the beautiful from the ugly, is intuitive, and it is customary to attribute it more especially to the female sex. Allowing this to be correct, an intuitive feeling for the beautiful is after all a talent, or, in other words, a natural capacity, which must be trained and educated under the influence of exterior influences. Furthermore, if correct taste is really oftener to be found in women than in men, the phenomenon can only be explained by the fact that in the ordinary course of life women are obliged to exercise their minds upon questions of taste much more frequently than men. Hence it seems evident that even in them taste is the result of practice and of training, rather than a natural gift.

If then taste, or rather the capacity of discerning and enjoying the beautiful, is a result of practice and training, and if it is coupled with an educational capacity, we must perforce acknowledge the extraordinary value of household art (which, being of a humble kind, is so often despised or looked upon as mere child's play), and consequently recognise the importance of woman's mission in the work of civilisation. The wife, while promoting the love of the beautiful through household art, and thus educating her own taste and that of her family, and her surroundings, becomes an active co-labourer in the education of the nation, and aids in general culture.

In our own day the task allotted to her is of even greater importance than in past times, when a correct feeling for art was a common inheritance and permeated society. All competent judges now unanimously agree that those branches of artistic activity in connection with which the word Taste is usually employed are in a most unsatisfactory state, and are only beginning to raise themselves by degrees from the decadent state into which they have fallen. Are artists and manufacturers, who have lost all feeling for and all comprehension of what is really beautiful or ugly, accountable for this state of things, or is the public, whose corrupt taste compels the artist to produce tasteless works, to be blamed for it?

We shall not enter upon further discussion of such questions, as the attempt to explain the present fall condition of these branches of art would carry us too far from our proper subject. We may, however, confidently assume that both are at fault, and we shall therefore, I think, do the public also a service, if we especially consider the present condition of domestic needlework. For my own peace of mind, I must preface my remarks by the words "present company always excepted", and ask my lady readers to believe that they are intended to be applied to all of them.

We may consider it as settled that it is woman's duty at the present time, not only to bring beauty into the house, but also to help to create it, and generally to assist in the revival of all the arts, by the education of taste and the cultivation of a feeling for the beautiful in herself and in all those who surround her. There are two special fields of activity in which she may profitably work toward this end, namely, domestic needlework and house decoration, and to these I desire to invite attention. I might add a third, namely, that of a woman's self-grooming in its entirety, for who will deny that care, attention and taste are as necessary in all matters appertaining to it as to anything else; for if a lady, while cultivating other branches of attraction, were to neglect this, she would be herself out of harmony to them in her own person, would destroy the picture which she had herself created. In point of fact she should be herself the noblest ornament of her ornamented dwelling.

How can I question, however, that in most ladies' houses all things are not ordered for the best, or suggest that everything in them is not so perfect that even the severest and most critical eyes can find no room for cavil. How can I doubt that ladies consciously or unconsciously are not thoroughly penetrated with the sentiment which inspired Ruckert's words – 'When the rose adorns herself, She adorns the garden'.

I am unfortunately unable to accord an equal measure of unreserved praise to domestic needlework, of which I shall at present mention only the most artistic, namely, embroidery, as time is wanting to discuss all its other endless varieties.

In the elucidation of the laws governing this branch of needlework, we shall, however, learn many lessons which may also be applied to the remaining branches. When looking at embroideries, we often cannot help observing that they show a disregard of the simplest laws of propriety, and that an immense amount of time, patience, trouble and most painstaking diligence have been wasted in reaching a paltry and sometimes even pitiable result. Having often observed a total ignorance of the simplest and most self-evident laws of decoration in work of this kind, together with an absence of reflection and a want of clear comprehension of means and ends, I feel that time will not be thrown away in considering it somewhat more carefully, and in the light of reason. The reform of tase by woman's agency can and should begin with embroidery, and the first and most imperative duty of her mission as a promoter of the beautiful is to improve it.

If I were looking for a collection of examples of bad work, I should only have to enter one of the shops where embroideries are sold, or to remember such an exhibition of woman's artistic work, as is annually held at the Volksgarten in Vienna, or to look over a few numbers of those richly illustrated journals which, together with prints of the fashions, also contain many patterns for domestic needlework. It would be unnecessary to consider such flagrant examples of misdirected ingenuity as the hollowing out of a statue of Venus with the intention of using it as a travelling-trunk or a violin-box, or as those which show us how an embroidered butterfly or a beetle or a slipper may be transformed into a watch-case. Good examples which have only lately begun to appear, are still few and far between, and are for the most part swamped in the mass of failures and absurdities. It is not my intention, however, to catalogue them. I only need to cite a few examples from whose peculiar errors some valuable lessons may be learnt.

I recollect hearing one of my friends, an artist, say that a lady once told him that she was making an embroidered portrait as a Christmas present for her husband. I cannot remember whether it was his likeness or hers, but at all events it was to be used to cover the seat of a chair. On his asking her whether she thought this a proper place for a portrait, she recognised her error and immediately sought a more fitting place for it. This shows that if the lady had not, like most people, been unaccustomed to reflect upon such matters, and had paused to think for an instant, she would never have fallen into so gross an error.

When we have once perceived that every object is not suited to every place, and that the proper place for any object must be determined by aesthetic considerations as well as by those of propriety, we shall be less likely to commit mistakes even in cases where the contradiction is less glaring than in the above instance. Pursuing the same train of thought we would now ask whether it is any less improper to lean against a portrait than to sit upon it. Since a portrait is unquestionably intended to be seen, and to remind us of the person whom it represents, we have no business to cover it up at all. How we do so is immaterial.

The lesson which we may learn from this example may be doubly profitable. What is true of the chair is also true of many other objects, for it is not the portrait only which may be a stumbling block of offence in cases of this kind. The art of the Baroque and Rococo period has bequeathed to us a fashion still in vogue, against which we feel obliged to protest. The manufacturers of Gobelin tapestries, who undertook to do with the loom what painters do with the brush, decorated chairs and sofas with all sorts of picture-subjects, treating their backs and seats as well-framed panels suitable for historical, allegorical, and genre subjects, and occasionally also for landscapes. This fashion was followed in embroidery, and has not yet been abandoned, though these subjects are as little fitted to such a purpose as portraits. They are objects of art which should be judged on their own merits, and when they are turned to common uses are certainly not intended to be covered up.

Modern embroiderers commit the same error when they apply such subjects to sofa-cushions, travelling-bags, footstools, head-rests and the like. We hang pictures upon the wall with the express intention of guarding them from touch. But in the cases named, we produce pictures with the intention of leaning our backs against them, of resting our heads upon them, and of trampling them underfoot. Do we think that we shall sit more comfortably with rocky landscapes at our backs, or that we shall sleep more soundly if we rest our heads upon loving couples holding sweet converse together, or that our feet will be the warmer if they repose upon embroidered pug-dogs?

These last specimens offer examples of still another mistake, which we may as well notice before going further. The subjects have not only been ill chosen, but they have been put in the wrong places. The principal decoration of a footstool ought not to occupy the place intended for the feet, where it will inevitably be soiled and rubbed off, but it should rather be put around the four sides, where the feet will not come in contact with it. If the upper surface is to be ornamented at all, the decorative pattern should be subdued, unobtrusive, purely conventional. Embroidered lamp-mats exhibit the same false treatment, for their chief ornament, a bouquet of flowers or whatever else it may be, is generally placed in the round central space. As this space is, however, invariably occupied by the lamp itself, the beautiful work put upon it can produce no effect whatsoever, and both the pains taken and the art expended are thrown away. Here also ornament should be concentrated upon the surrounding border, which always remains visible. If we keep these examples and the lessons which they teach in our minds, they will guide us aright in many similar cases. As something yet remains to be said about embroidered figures and pictures, we must return to them for a moment. If we call recent exhibitions to mind, we shall remember to have seen many large pieces of embroidery, representing figure-subjects stretched on frames in such a manner as to show that they were not intended for any practical use, but as independent works of art, like pictures. Their aim, their purpose, the only excuse indeed for their existence, is the same as that of the pictures which they aspire to imitate, namely, beauty. If we regard them from this point of view, and examine the blending of the colours, the flow of the lines, the beauty of the faces, the expression of character, and whatever else would be apt to invite criticism in a painting, do we find anything in them calculated to give us the slightest satisfaction? Can these colours, however beautiful in themselves, ever be blended together, separated as they are by hard straight lines? Can these outlines be graceful, elegant, and flowing, worked as they are in cross-stitch by the combination of rows of small rectangular points? Is it in any way possible, with such limited means at command, to give beauty of form to the heads, or to express such emotions as pleasure, sorrow, love, hate, anger, etc, and when this is attempted can the result be other than the most complete caricature?

For these reasons it often happens that the artist, finding it impossible to embroider the heads, gives up the attempt in despair, and cutting them out of the lithograph before her, sews them into her work. This, however, only makes bad worse. Lithographs are not, in themselves, considered to be of much artistic value, so that the insertion thus made is worthless. Furthermore, the materials combined disagree with each other, the one being soft, pliable, and yet firm, the other fragile in the highest degree, easily torn, and sure to be destroyed by cleaning. Finally, the artist, by adopting this expedient, makes public display of her own artistic incompetency. If figures and heads are to be repeated – and we do not by any means intend to say that the art of embroidery is unable to deal with them – they should also be worked with the needle, but in a stitch which will produce satisfactory results. Our ordinary cross-stitch and point-work are absolutely unfitted for the purpose, and bead-work is, if possible, still worse.

What are the artistic peculiarities of the various kinds of embroidery now generally practised by amateurs, so called, as I beg to assure my readers, to distinguish those who work for their own pleasure from professional needlewomen? Small squares are combined, mosaic-fashion, to form straight lines and angles. However fine the work, however small the squares, the principle is still the same. Any design, therefore, which is not made up of straight lines, can never be satisfactorily executed in this way, and any pattern containing curved instead of broken lines is unsuitable, and its use if a blunder. It follows that all representations of figures and landscapes are inadmissible, and that only designs composed of straight lines, on a geometric basis, such as the meander or Greek fret, are allowable. Anything else is objectionable, unless in cases where the work is destined to be seen at a sufficient distance to make the zigzag lines appear continuous. Even naturalistic representations of flowers, although most frequently chosen as subjects, are unfit to be executed in embroidery of this kind, as Nature nowhere makes use of straight lines or of continually recurring zigzags.

The range of ornament applicable to embroidered work of this kind is therefore extremely limited, but it is still of sufficient importance to make it worth while not to abandon it altogether, more especially as it has this advantage, that any women of moderately educated taste and a slight measure of inventive genius can make her own designs, and thus emancipate herself from current patterns and models, which are bad as a rule. The purpose of this ornamentation, as indeed of all decoration, is beauty of outward appearance, although this is but seldom reached by such simple means. The object is to produce regularly distributed, beautiful, and harmonious combinations of colour, quiet or rich in effect, as the case may be, and this is not beyond the reach of an amateur of practised and cultivated taste.

If we desire to pass beyond this stage of decorative composition, and represent freely drawn ornaments, natural or conventionalised flowers, or figure-subjects and the like, we must give up amateur methods, and take to those of a more artistic character. In the fifteenth century, when embroidery was a real art, and almost a rival of painting, the methods now generally adopted were hardly known. They first became popular when the decline of embroidery had set in. The flat stitch was formerly exclusively used for the representation of faces and hands, and this is without doubt the only correct method, as it allows of free and artistic work because the threads can be laid so as to follow the drawing. It gives the workman as complete control of his needle as the artist has of his brush. Only when thus treated can embroidery be raised to the rank of needle-painting, and render even biblical subjects in an acceptable manner. In the subordinate parts, such as large flat spaces and groundwork, other methods, which produce a more even surface, may, however, be used, and were indeed used by the embroiderers of the fifteenth and sixteenth centuries. This is more especially necessary when threads of gold, which amateurs do not at all know how to manage, although they are exceedingly rich in decorative effect, are employed. In general, it may be said that a lady who desires to solve the higher and more difficult problems in the art of embroidery must be well acquainted with all the many technical processes involved, and must know when and where to employ each of them. The male and female artists of the Middle Ages followed this course, and none other is followed in the Persian, Indian, Chinese, and Japanese embroideries. These, however Baroque their subjects and ornaments may be, far exceed all similar productions of modern European civilisation in perfection of workmanship, in display of technical skill, and above all in decorative effect, which is after all the real end and aim of this kind of work. While, therefore, we frequently fall into error by giving no thought to the subject and the place where it properly belongs, it happens but too often that, owing to technical insufficiency, we waste all our trouble and labour, and leave the observer room for no other thought than regret for the eyes which have been ruined, and the time and diligence wasted which might have been more worthily bestowed. Besides the mistakes made in selection, and the insufficiency of technical methods shown in execution, we meet with other errors and perversions of skill which can also be attributed only to thoughtlessness. Of these I shall again take an actual example as an illustration, which is by no means isolated, but rather a type of a whole class.

This example is an imitation of a well-known engraving, worked upon white silk in the finest black silk thread. The delicacy of workmanship, the drawing, the shading, and the modelling are all exquisite, although the black drawing on the silk somewhat heightens the effect of the embroidery. I do not, however, intend to find fault with it on this score, but to confine myself to the objection that the aim and the whole artistic tendency of the work are false.

What task did the artist set herself? Evidently to copy an engraving. Her utmost possibility was consequently to equal the engraving in beauty.

Granting that she has done so what was the use of employing such an unspeakable amount of diligence and labour, and expending so much skill upon a single copy, while the original print could be multiplied from the copperplate in untold numbers, easily, cheaply, and in silk if that were desired? As far as the beauty of any representation is concerned, the technical process employed is valuable only as a means, and the knowledge that the work has been done with the needle adds nothing whatever to its artistic value. Technical processes have an independent value of their own, and their employment is justified in so far only as they offer peculiar advantages, and enable us to do something which cannot be done as well, or in a more practical shape, by other processes.

Now embroidery does offer such advantages. It is painting with the needle, and its special element is colour — another consideration which was entirely overlooked by the person who made the abovementioned copy of an engraving in black and white. Although it is true that embroidery cannot pretend to rival painting in the height of its aims, it still has its peculiar excellences, which are derived from beauty of material, power and depth of colour, and the brilliant gloss of silk. Its special quality is that, being itself pliable, it can apply painting to pliable objects. That is its proper domain, into which painting cannot and should not enter, and which it shares with weaving only. Embroidery may therefore be very well content to leave picture-making to painting.

From all this it follows that embroidery is not really a free and independent, but rather a decorative art. It ornaments and decorates objects which are intended for practical use, and adds to them the element of beauty. The artist must constantly remember that what she represents, what she works with her needle, is not the really important matter, so much as the giving of the most suitable decoration possible to the object for which her work is undertaken. Her choice is therefore not untrammelled, but fettered by that object. She must ask herself, not what is abstractly beautiful, or what pleases her best, but what will best decorate the object under consideration, and is most suitable to it.

This question, which she should ask herself, will guard her against many errors, and will save her much fruitless toil and labour. She will be brought to consider how her task may be accomplished with the least possible trouble, and to select for this purpose the technical method calculated to insure the quickest, simplest, and most effective results.

This leads us to remark that it is a great mistake to suppose that the aesthetical value of an object is in any way determined by the amount of labour expended upon it or the technical difficulties overcome in adorning it. On the contrary, in art the artificial is inadmissible; the simpler and plainer the means, the higher the success attained through them will be valued. What a tedious piece of work it is to fill large spaces, or backgrounds, with minute stitches, and yet a piece of silk or woollen stuff of the same colour would serve precisely the same purpose!

I have used this last illustration with the direct intention of calling attention to the Oriental use of applied embroidery, which, being well fitted for larger objects, would enable ladies, with but little trouble, to gradually fill their dwellings with the most beautiful and effective pieces of ornament, such as covers, curtains, pillows, cushions, and the like, and at the same time give them an easy, pleasant, and in no wise tedious occupation. I may assume that this kind of work is well known, especially as examples are here and there to be seen, such as chair-coverings, cushions, and footstools. I allude to the sewing on of variously coloured pieces of woollen stuffs of velvet or silk, to a coloured ground, with outlines embroidered in colour. The design must of course be beautiful, and the colouring harmonious. These elements are quite sufficient to reach the end aimed at, which is simply to produce an agreeable decorative effect. The pieces may also be combined mosaic fashion, as in Persian covers, but this sort of work is more difficult and troublesome.

These remarks have already brought me within the second of those fields of activity which I have already designated as especially allotted to woman in the following out of her aesthetic mission. This second field is the artistically harmonious adornment of her house, which depends partly upon her handiwork and partly upon her choice of objects.

It is hardly necessary for me to point out in detail where and how universally the hand of woman can make itself felt in the embellishment of the house. There can be no doubt that every lady desires (although there may often be reasons which prevent her from doing so) to decorate the rooms in which she lives with the work of her own hands, and to make otherwise vacant places attractive to the eye by some pleasing object. We know also from daily experience that the feminine mind is very intelligent in such matters. In spite of all this our dwellings continually show us mistakes committed, toil and labour expended upon useless and unmeaning knick-knacks, or wasted, often on a large scale, in wrong places. I will not again speak of offences against style in embroidery, but will content myself with citing such examples only as lamp-mats and footstools, to which artistic decoration is applied in places where it either cannot be seen at all, or else is condemned to be ignominiously soiled and destroyed. Artistic productions of this class are made to be seen; their end and aim is beauty of outward appearance, and appearance is for the eye. On the other hand, we must not forget that domestic utensils are for practical use and not for show, and that they must therefore combine utility with beauty.

It also seems to me, generally speaking, that embroidery is used altogether too little in the decoration of the dwelling, and that, whenever it is so employed, it is happened by unnecessary difficulties, resulting from the tedious technical methods adopted. This might easily be avoided. As an example of it, take those comparatively large rugs worked in cross-stitch with Berlin wool, whose delicate nature, want of thickness and strength, made them ill adapted to the purposes for which they are intended; for although diligent and nimble fingers have been at work upon them for months, and sometimes even for years, they are rapidly worn out. One cannot help regretting the time, toil, and labour expended upon them, when he considers that rugs which are artistically as well as practically superior to them can be woven with less trouble and in a much simpler manner. Embroidery is a delicate art, unfit for the decoration of large surfaces. When however, it undertakes such a task, it must do so in a certain sense from the point of view of monumental art, and instead of spreading pieces of embroidery on the floor and under our feet, must adapt them to places where they will be protected.

Even for small mats, backcloths, pillows, cushions, and chair-covers, cross-stitch and point-work are, as a rule, too tedious and time-consuming processes. Think only of the variety of objects which might be executed in the time saved by the adoption of some simpler technical method, capable of yielding equally satisfactory artistic results! How easy to decorate lambrequins, curtains of all kinds, rugs and covers, and cords; how rich the effects that may be produced on them by applied embroidery, provided only that we know what is wanted, and are convinced that it is not the labour expended upon an object which determines its artistic value, but its beauty as a result.

It is, however, absolutely necessary that in all cases there should be a perfectly clear comprehension of the aim to be reached, for in work of this kind nothing must be done for its own sake, no pattern selected simply for its beauty, and no colour because it happens to please, for otherwise it will often happen that the pattern or the colour, when fixed in its place, not being in harmony with its surroundings, will ruin all our good intentions. It is evident, therefore, that to attain a good result all things must be selected and made with reference, not only to the places they are intended to decorate, but with reference also to the complete artistic harmony of their surroundings. This, of course, demands an artistically trained eye, capable of taking in at a glance the aesthetic possibilities of a given space, and of using them so as to make them conduce to the general artistic harmony. It is not sufficient to know that red harmonises with green, and orange with blue, but we must also be able to say, in this place we shall need red, in that yellow, in that blue, so as to fill the void, to relieve and light up what is sombre, and to produce everywhere the best and most appropriate effect.

Such an eye for harmony and for colour is, of course, not very often to be met with, and to this fact may perhaps be attributed a very common error noticeable in our dwellings, the preponderance, namely, of white. We do , indeed, upholster our furniture with costly, lustrous, and richly coloured fabrics, but we conceal them under white covers. Of what use is a thing of beauty to its possessor if its beauty is to be so hidden that it cannot be enjoyed? For this reason the white "tidies" which we spread out on the backs of chairs and sofas, though useful, are objectionable, as they for the most part hide the colour of the furniture under white frilly spots which destroy all aesthetic effect. Their destructive power is greater in proportion to the deeper or stronger tones of walls and furniture. As we have given up colour in other objects, so also have we banished it from our household linen, and especially from that used on the table. It is indeed true that neatness and cleanliness in the house are good things, and that in this they find their highest expression; but nevertheless it is not necessary to carry puritanism about colour to the extent to which it has been carried in this particular. There are aesthetic reasons enough why we should do well to use colour for the decoration of linen, as in past times. We might adorn table and bed in a variety of charming ways, and thus provide constant employment for female hands, whose works would be a daily source of fresh delight to the eye. The lady of the house will more especially have need of an aesthetically trained eye and an all-embracing judgment, where she does not work with her own hand, but is called upon to act in matters where selection and artistic direction are concerned, such as in the decoration of walls, the selection of colours, of furniture, and of carpets, as well as the arrangement, position, and distribution of the various household objects. As the mistress of the house, she must accustom herself to look upon her rooms in all their details as pictures in which all things are so placed and combined as to contribute to the general artistic effect. Symmetry should not be too pronounced in a picture, and yet a conscious arrangement should make itself felt through main groups and subordinate groups, balance of masses, distribution of light and shade, harmony of colours, united by the predominance of a general hue. So should it be in a dwelling. There, also, no one object exists for itself alone, but in reference to all other objects. If the lady of the house has accustomed herself to view things in this light she will soon perceive where there is a discord and where perfect harmony is attained: she will be able to recognise the chief place which ought to dominate the rest; to see where there is too much or too little; where there is a gap needing to be filled up with some object or work of art; what object is superfluous, or ought to be removed because it is out of proportion with its surroundings; where and how this or that piece of work may be used to best advantage. She will soon become capable of deciding which hues and tints she may select in harmony with her individual taste for walls and furniture, and which other hues may be contrasted with these fundamental colours of the decoration so as to produce the best possible effect. This is by no means an easy task, for whose success or failure the mistress of the house must be held responsible. The different impressions which house interiors make upon us are mainly due to the presence or the absence of this capacity of the eye, this feeling for harmony, this sensibility to artistic effect. We enter a sumptuously furnished drawing-room, wanting neither in gilding, in heavy silks, nor marbles and alabasters, and lo! The atmosphere seems as heavy as lead, a chill runs through out veins, and the hand, or rather the fingers, stretched out towards us, appears to be offered in compliance with the laws of politeness and the customs of society, but not from any prompting of the heart. We enter another dwelling which has no trace of the wealth and luxury of the first, and yet a sense of comfort steals over us; we feel the hearty pressure of the hand even before it touches our own, we are convinced that we are welcome, and cannot bear to depart. Why is this? It is because a poetical, intelligence mind has been at work here, and has united warm, pleasant hues of colour in cheerful harmony – a gentle, amiable person, who has the faculty of making herself and others comfortable, has so arranged the chairs and other pieces of furniture that they invite to conversation; has agreeably filled corners, walls and tables with flowers and plants and with works of love and of art, modest though they may be. There, on the contrary, fashion only has been consulted; the upholsterer has undertaken to furnish the house, he has followed his usual insipid routine without consulting the wishes and feelings of the gentleman and the lady of the house, who have had nothing to say in the matter, either because they did not understand it, or did not think it worth the trouble to consider it. This latter mode of proceeding may be said to be the rule in the furnishing of the more pretentious class of apartments. By adopting it, however, we not only deprive ourselves of an agreeable and pleasurable occupation, but we also renounce all certainty of success, as the artisan and the decorator are dependent upon fashion, and the fashion of today, at least, is indifferent to beauty.

It is true that there are upholsterers and decorative artists who rise above fashion and can both understand and carry out artistic intentions. But if we are not ourselves able to appreciate them, to recognise and to value that which is truly good and tasteful, we shall find, like a certain lady whom we have in mind, that even with the best of will, with good intentions and copious means, our efforts have ended in nothing but annoyance and vexation. This lady desired to accomplish something in the decoration and furnishing of her new grand drawing rooms which should rise above the ordinary level of modern tastelessness, and for this purpose addressed herself to the best workmen, and unfortunately not only to one but to several. Being herself without knowledge and judgement in such matters, and incapable of deciding between different views and aims, now taking advice from one and then from the other, and following neither, she was in a perpetually discontented, wavering state of mind. Having caused the costly painted ceiling to be taken down because it did not suit the wallpaper, and changed the wallpaper because the furniture did not harmonise with it, she finally reached an unsatisfactory result, which gave pleasure neither to herself nor to others.

This illustration shows us that the ideal mission of woman, as a promotor of the beautiful, has also its practical subjective side. The want of a feeling for beauty occasionally brings heavy retribution, and this is another reason, which added to those of an ideal nature, should lead us to develop it with special care. We now know, if we remember what has been said, that modern culture indispensably demands the fostering of a sense of beauty in ourselves; that it is necessary for the sake of the education of our children, whose aesthetic perceptions are generally corrupted from early infancy by bad picture-books and tasteless surroundings; we know that in cultivating this feeling for beauty we are doing our part towards working out the civilisation of the future, little as the part may be which any individual can contribute towards it; and finally we know that it will open up to us a source of pleasure and of enjoyment during the whole of our lives. These are surely reasons enough to make us attach the highest importance to woman's aesthetic mission. Let us not, however, be led to suppose that the comprehension of the beautiful will come of itself; on the contrary, toil and practice will be required, and this all the more for the reason that we do not grow up in the midst of beautiful things as our predecessors did, who lived in happier art-epochs, and because our taste is perverted by the present fashions in dress, in industries, and even in art. The beautiful has a language of its own, and this language must be learned like any other. He, however, who has learned it, and knows how to use it, has – to borrow the language of Goethe – tasted of that nectar which Minerva brought down from Heaven to her favourite Prometheus, and thus has his part in the highest happiness – in Art.

A note about Boom Publications Ltd

We are a more-than-profit eco-publisher, donating the majority of our profits towards educational scholarships for underprivileged students. We help graduates and academics make their mark on the world - we push the boundaries, share brilliant ideas and inspire possibility. We plant trees for every commissioned book sold, and give our authors the chance to profit-share from their brilliant ideas. Through academic excellence and environmental sustainability, *Boom Graduates* are changing the world.

Thank you for contributing by purchasing this book. Please visit our catalogues on www.boompublications.com and get in touch with helen@boompublications.com for advice on publication.

Jacob Von Falke and Helen Gorrill

Notes

Jacob Von Falke and Helen Gorrill

Woman's Aesthetic Mission

Jacob Von Falke and Helen Gorrill

Woman's Aesthetic Mission

Jacob Von Falke and Helen Gorrill

Woman's Aesthetic Mission

Jacob Von Falke and Helen Gorrill

Woman's Aesthetic Mission

Jacob Von Falke and Helen Gorrill

Woman's Aesthetic Mission

www.ingramcontent.com/pod-product-compliance
Lightning Source LLC
Chambersburg PA
CBHW070305220526
45465CB00004B/1754